My Day in the Office

By Alex Kimathi

Illustrated by Anton Syadrov

Library For All Ltd.

Here is the desk where I work.

Here is my chair.

Here is the printer.

Here is the telephone.

Here is my computer.

Here are my files.

Here is my notebook.

Here is my laptop.

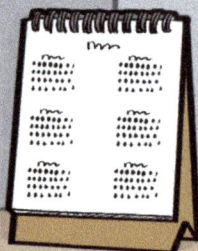

Here is the whiteboard.

Here is my calendar.

Here are the office supplies.

Here is my coffee.

Here is my team.

We have a meeting.

Sometimes, we have
a workshop.

This is my office.

I come here to work every day.

About the contributors

Library For All works with authors and illustrators from around the world to develop diverse, relevant, high-quality books. Visit libraryforall.org for the latest news on writers' workshop events, submission guidelines and other creative opportunities.

Did you enjoy this book?

We have hundreds more expertly curated original stories to choose from.

We work in partnership with authors, educators, cultural advisors, governments and NGOs to bring the joy of reading to people everywhere.

Did you know?

We create global impact in these fields by embracing the United Nations Sustainable Development Goals.

libraryforall.org

You're reading Level 1

Learner – Beginner readers

Start your reading journey with short words, big ideas and plenty of pictures.

Level 1 – Rising readers

Raise your reading level with more words, simple sentences and exciting images.

Level 2 – Eager readers

Enjoy your reading time with familiar words, but complex sentences.

Level 3 – Progressing readers

Develop your reading skills with creative stories and some challenging vocabulary.

Level 4 – Fluent readers

Step up your reading skills with playful narratives, new words and fun facts.

Level 5 – Curious readers

Discover your world through science and stories.

Level 6 – Adventurous readers

Explore your world through science and stories.

Library For All is an Australian not for profit organisation with a mission to make knowledge accessible to all via an innovative digital library solution. Visit us at libraryforall.org

My Day in the Office

First published 2024

Published by Library For All Ltd
Email: info@libraryforall.org
URL: libraryforall.org

This project was delivered with the support of Edmund Rice Foundation Australia.

Edmund Rice
FOUNDATION AUSTRALIA
Liberating Lives Through Education

Original illustrations by Anton Syadrov

My Day in the Office
Kimathi, Alex
ISBN: 978-1-923339-60-6
SKU04520